Congrats Superwoman

When You've Climbed the Mountain and
Still Don't Feel Good Enough

Alisia Young

Eat 'N' Live Free Publishing

Eat 'N' Live Free Publishing
PO Box 66105 Town Centre
Pickering, ON L1V 6P7
support@eatnlivefree.com
www.eatnlivefree.com

Book Layout © 2020 BookDesignTemplates.com

Cover photo by: Noel Photography

Cover design by: 100Covers

Congrats Superwoman : when you've climbed the mountain and still don't feel good enough/ Alisia Young. -- 1st ed.

ISBN 978-1-7774198-1-3

Dedication

For my coaches, who have guided me along the way, and my supportive and ever-loving family and friends, who have each contributed to my growth in one way or another. I hope all of you take solace and relish in well-deserved enjoyment, for it is all of you who are impacting others through your impact on me.

And for all my clients, your trust in me to walk alongside you is an honor I hold highly. I am so proud of each and every one of you, and am ecstatic for what's to come.

Table of Contents

Preface

Thank you for picking up this book and deciding to spend some time together with me.

This book has been on my heart for several years, yet the Covid-19 pandemic of 2020 has given me the much-needed sense of urgency to get it out on the market so that the content can readily reach those who need it.

Although this book is written as somewhat of a memoir, I'd like this to be a valuable personal experience for you, and have provided you with a set of questions to reflect on.

You can access the reflective questions, along with other supportive materials at www.congratssuperwoman.com.

I'd also love to hear about your experience of reading this book, so feel free to reach out to me if you feel moved to.

Lastly, names mentioned in the book, except for the author and the names listed in the acknowledgments section, have been changed.

Without further ado, let's get right into it!

PART 1:

FEELING BEHIND IN LIFE DESPITE HAVING DONE WHAT I "SHOULD" HAVE TO GET AHEAD

Quarter-Life Existential Crisis:
Bankruptcy And Student Loan Debt

There was a very false sense of security that became a close companion as I went down the path of "borrow now, pay it later"—the typical paradigm brought upon by student loan accumulation birthed from the pursuit and promise of higher education. When signing up for my first loan via the Ontario Student Assistance Program at the naïve age of 17, I gave in to a baseless hopefulness; one that told of how quickly I would be able to pay it off within a few years of graduating, and that I'd love every moment of the educational process. I knew it would be challenging, I was—after all—treading into unknown territory. Nonetheless, I was encouraged by those around me, and found myself personally believing the mantra I then paid homage to: I could figure it out along the way.

The alluring security of "live now, you can easily pay it back later," meant not constantly limiting myself and being worried sick about my financial decisions and situation. So, whether I was getting a bus pass, living outside of home, or getting a gym membership (as I could aptly rationalize these as important for my well-being, and by extension, my future ability to help others), I wasn't thinking about the little things that add up, nor those little details in the fine print—such as simple fees and interest charges. Why bother keeping a budget when I'll easily be profiting from the fruits of my labor soon enough? To top it off, I'd be doing it while positively impacting the world through educating others with regards to their health. Life was looking up, or so I thought.

When I filed for bankruptcy in March 2020, I felt like a failure in more ways than I initially thought possible. Even before graduating in 2018, I was barely reaching my minimums for my credit cards and line of credit. How, then, was I maxed out despite working multiple jobs and not living a lavish, over-the-top lifestyle?

Two years after completing my education and still having these nagging reminders of what I owed weighed on me like a never-ending burden. At first, I didn't even allow myself the time to properly assess the severity of my situation.

Deciding to file for bankruptcy was a true blessing in disguise. It forced me to pause, and see the reality of the situation I've landed in; rather than just running, running and running—in a feeble attempt to remedy my plight without properly thinking things through. I needed to sternly sit myself down and meditate on the things that mattered: what I desired for my future; whether to keep paying for past mistakes and decisions, or to take the chance and really think about what I needed to do differently, and how I want to turn my life around going forward.

The Word "Should" Instigates A Visceral Reaction Whenever I Hear It

This word is downright harmful, simply for its telling of a person in the way they ought to live their life. It's a person pushing their agenda on to another sentient, free-thinking being. Something I've noticed as I've gone through life is that despite some people being genuinely well-meaning at heart, there are those that have questionable intentions, masked by a wholesome façade during their presentations of such intent.

There've been countless conversations in which I've had people tell me I should be doing this or that, all of which surfaced without any provocation or request on my part.

For example, one evening after wrapping up a health seminar I had offered to the members of a gym, I crossed paths with a colleague whose fitness classes I had participated in—and even covered for—whilst studying to become a Naturopathic Doctor. At the time, I was finally what one would consider as having been successfully inaugurated into the community. I was sharing education and having health dialogues while building my practice.

While briefly reconnecting with my colleague, she introduced me to her friend who was with her. Upon sharing that I was at the beginning stages of building my practice, which entailed preserving a few days for my practice and working in other roles to generate the income to finance my practice, she proceeded to advise me to reach out to other clinics in the city to work as a Naturopath for them. She advised me. On her own account. She didn't ask if I was interested in her perhaps making a suggestion...but advised me right away, as though she had a vested interest in the success or failure of my business. As though we had not just met three minutes prior, and made the impression on me that she was not aware that I likely had my own plan or vision for myself, nor that working elsewhere might've been something I considered prior to our conversation, but did not want to do for whatever reasons I may have had.

This made me wonder if—unbeknownst to me—I've been walking around with a huge question mark hovering over my head. More often than not, their imposing of views are not in the very least welcome. I had in no way desired their commentary. But my personal aim to be accepting, as well as hopeful, to the chance that these people are telling me such things with the best of intentions, enables me to do my best in letting it slide—while, at the back of my head, knowing that they were more than likely projecting themselves on me.

I continue to wonder what compels others to vomit their agenda and values unto others. If it's, innocently, a coincidence that happens frequently; or if these are just natural manifestations of personality traits widespread in society; or if it's something I'm radiating that makes others feel so comfortable doing so. On certain days, I can't help but wonder…

Am I Living Life Properly?

At this stage of my life, I feel behind. I should be married, or engaged. At the very least, I should be dating somebody, no? It gets even more difficult when I see those I grew up with having these very things going on in their lives; and although I'm truly excited for them, I can't help but worry: am I going to be left behind? Even though this phase presents itself as a valuable time to get certain things in order and really focus on myself, there's still a daunting fear of the unknown that I can't seem to shake off. Will I ever get what I feel I deserve? Is thinking that way me being entitled?

When it comes to the desire to have kids, I question myself on where I stand. Deep, deep down, I do desire children, the whole package actually. Being married, having a beautiful home with my own personal zoo of loving pets… Yet, when I see the happenings of this world, I find myself questioning if I can handle it. Seeing the inherent inequality and unfairness that persists, why would I willingly bring someone into that? When a successful marriage is dependent on myself and an ever changing—hopefully, evolving—other individual, do I really want to spend my energy—and my life—working on that? What if I have a son? Would I then be okay with constantly worrying about his safety, which is threatened solely because he exists? And what if I have a daughter? How can I ensure that I equip her with sufficient resources to immerse herself in developing a healthy sense of self-worth and relationship IQ to surround herself with endearing relationships and steer clear when faced with red flags?

It's funny, as these dreams are what drove me to pursue an investment into higher education in the first place. I believed that such a path would provide me with the means to achieve all of those things and not be shaken. Yet, the things I was so sure I wanted, back when I was 17, are the very things I question with regards to their ability to provide me with a sense of wholeness, or if they will end up entailing way more stress than I'm willing to deal with.

This reminds me of one of my friends and colleagues who, during a conversation, managed to make me feel safe enough to share that I wasn't sure if I'd want to have kids after graduating. The look of surprise on his face surprised me. Shortly after realizing that I was being serious, he defensively stated the importance of having children, especially by virtue of being so seemingly maternal by nature. Yet, while seeming to try to convince me of the mistake I'm making by seriously considering to not procreate, he hadn't shared anything about the reality of his life situation: of pursuing school full-time while his wife provided the primary care needs for their daughter.

I'm also reminded of a childhood friend who gave me a look of confusion; an expression that clearly questioned: "are you out of your mind?!" This happened after she nonchalantly made a comment regarding a distant unseen future where we have children, and I, just as nonchalantly, responded that I'm not sure if I want to have children.

But see here, she had a stable job, and was in a long term relationship which seemed to be on the trajectory of marriage. And to her, I must've been out of my mind to think that I might not want to have kids, especially while still single. Thing is, I was focused on getting this debt paid down, and figuring out where I'm personally going in my life before bringing a being into the chaos. Afterall, they deserve nothing but the best attention and focus.

The point I'd like to make from these examples is this: oftentimes, when people converse, it can feel more comfortable to believe that someone you consider a friend has the same perspective as you, on things that are wrongly assumed to be "givens" in life.

An Outside Opinion Is Not Necessarily Your Inner Truth

For me, a "should" that's especially been a point of contention since graduating is that I should want to be in my field full-time, and it's only going to take a certain amount of time to become profitable through practicing, and that my passion which left before graduating will inevitably return; someday, somehow.

A specific critic in my life whom I've always wanted to gain the approval of (due to our skewed power dynamic present from the onset of our relationship) told me how messed up it was that I was not practicing what I went to school for, and proceeded to tell me what I should do and what the successful people he knew would do.

This speaks to the plain ignorance of the fact that, just because somebody goes to school for a long time in pursuit of a certain career, does not mean that they're guaranteed to be profitable in that area, nor that they will enjoy it and continue to see it as their life's calling till kingdom come. Are we not allowed to change? When I went into Naturopathy, I didn't know it would be about becoming an entrepreneur.

When I visualized my future, I imagined days filled with educating and inspiring others to make changes in their lives to transform themselves. To break free from the chains of generational traumas and the consequences they entailed, such as diseases spawned by un-serving lifestyle habits, and lack of discernment around nutritional wisdom (along with that of political agendas and their impacts on societal behavioral norms, of course).

People who freely comment on how others should be living their lives are not thinking about the things people in the dumps are busy struggling with—for me, that was staying afloat and being a single woman, all while desiring to settle down and enjoy a certain degree of financial stability.

There's so much I didn't know then that I know now, which were only learned through taking the path I decided to tread.

Questioning My Identity And Path

Vividly, I remember urgently wanting to grow up since I was six. It seemed like that would be when life would officially "begin". I also remember having a very serious nature and often being that one person out of the bunch who was always overly cautious and thinking further ahead, that one who never stayed in the moment, and never basked in the blessing of youth.

My contemplation upon this leads me to question: Exactly when did I start to have the concept of an identity; an awareness of my standing in this physical world and dimension, along with where society ranks me before I have a say? The gap between the social standing delegated to me and my own reality was too damn big. The former subconsciously denoted what I believed my limitations are, how high my ceilings go.

Thinking back, some of my greatest memories of when my identity was formed was based on who I grew up with and spent the most time with. For most of my childhood I grew up around my brother, cousins, school mates, and the ever-reliable TV and books (the Internet became a bigger deal later).

I don't remember the exact moment it happened, but I know that it was before I was ten years old. I looked at my dominant personality traits of being very quiet, "nice" (as I was told, which I now interpret as mild and non-threatening), studious. These were traits I accepted as me, as unchanging. I recall being a bookworm was constantly focused on and celebrated, which led my impressionable sense of self to believe, and cling to developing this, because it would be my ticket to a happy life. From then, I relied on developing my intelligence and helpful nature to connect with others and to drive ahead. This further intertwined with the importance for me of having a certain title to establish my status with, such as that of a Doctor, and that's where my identity became rooted in that title.

Set On A Track Without Really Knowing

I wonder what was fueling and driving me at that time. It started as early as when I was back in high school, and being on the academic track as opposed to an applied one, and just following these crumbs to wherever they led. At that time, the academic track was the only viable trajectory for getting into a university, and the applied track was geared towards striving for a college education or going straight to work after.

Here's the thing, beyond the academic route, laid the "golden" careers that were highly raved about and sought after. Thus, not much of my time was spent investigating alternate paths. Now, however, I see the beauty in that "leap" year. Though it was low-key frowned upon while in school, what a lovely time in life it is to give yourself time to grow more and become clearer on your desired future, especially if it's a little clouded. It definitely beats rushing along a path only to find out 4 to 10+ years in, and $40K to $200K+ deep that if you had just taken a pause amongst the tidal wave encouraging you to move along faster, that you might've chosen a different path more in line with what makes sense for you.

With 20/20 hindsight, I wish I had encouraged myself at the time to be more patient. But at the same time, sometimes it is these unfitting twists and turns that lead us to where we need to be, and once there, we claim that space with an extra amount of conviction and vengeance. Anyhow, I've met less than five people in my life so far who can say that they knew with 100% certainty what they wanted for themself in the last year of high school, and what would be important to them.

But higher education meant higher tuition fees. The attitude towards this dilemma, among most—or at least those who voiced it—was simple: that if you and your family don't have the money to pursue a higher education, and you're eligible to take up student loans, then, by all means, take those loans. Life is short, you don't have much time, and you can worry about paying it off later. Looking back, (even though I don't encourage living in the realms of the past), I can see that it would've been helpful to approach the route of seeking higher education from the standpoint of pursuing a venture with a combination of one's natural talents, areas of interests, and where there is a demand for one's services.

Unfortunately, back then, I was chasing a vehicle for financial security, along with status and respect. I ventured into naturopathic medicine because I truly believed in the philosophy. Besides, the idea of doing on-calls and multiple days of overnight shifts in the conventional medical model did not resonate with me. When I imagined what I viewed as healing, it included deep talks one-on-one, education and prevention as empowerment, and the knowledge of targeted natural prescriptions at my disposal, which would supplement fundamental transformation through addressing and tightening up one's health hygiene. It also involved having a team of experts in all the fields of health and coaching, with each specialty working holistically to support the individual in the center to achieve their best self in mind, body, and spirit.

You Learn When You Dive In

There are things that weren't even on my radar to look into, such as licensing exam fees, loans, and the whole feat of getting a business up, as well as running it afterwards. I also learned that there often come breaking points where it's questionable to continue pushing forward—where it's exceptionally hard to make a decision because of the investments already made, along with the promise of potential, and the resilience built from previous obstacles which were overcome to reach said point.

I learned this during my training, while trying to juggle back-to-back classes, working part-time, and trying to hide, explain away, and justify an eating disorder. All while needing to redo a few courses due to the performance anxiety experienced during the previous bout of practical exams, and pressure to not fail again so as to not be escorted out of the program. Most days, I was kicking myself in the back of my head with the regret of not performing and not trusting myself, even though I knew the answers.

However, there's no way to know it all before taking that leap of faith. I recall colleagues I met in the program who mentioned they had never seen an ND before, yet heard about the program and profession, and pressed "GO" as all they needed to know is that they were all for it. Meanwhile, I shadowed an ND (who opened my eyes to the profession), toured the school years before applying, organized my university courses in a strategic manner years before applying, and viewed the schedule, read up as much as I could, and saw an intern at the clinic, all before gaining acceptance to the program. I had the academic side all figured out, yet missed the 8-ball that is the financial aspect of it all.

Yet, at that point in time in my educational career, that was the absolute best I could've done. And as I compassionately remind my clients when they dig themselves back into a sense of regret, I too practice self-compassion and remind myself of the same.

Regardless, if I knew of the future impact, what I would have done differently is to take a personal finance course in university. In fact, just as how intro-level courses are a standard before deciding on the direction(s) of one's degree, I do advocate that taking a personal finance course should be essential in our instituted learning; in both high school and college/university levels.

I can see how I would've made a lot of different decisions, if I had known about the impact of interest rates on loans, alongside balancing that with working multiple entry-level jobs to make income while attaining my license and building a business. And how that would impact how quickly I could contribute to other goals and dreams which weren't as urgent at the time, but definitely of interest, such as home-ownership, contributing towards a strong retirement, and the nipping fees that come up such as insurance, business-building, health, and leisure.

I am grateful to say that although I can't change the past decisions with the wisdom in current day, I can say with confidence that the result has pushed me today in a way that I don't think I'd hunger as much had things turned out ideally.

Chapter 3

Impulsive, Insecurity-Filled Actions With No Regard For The Bigger Picture

I found myself seeking ways to feel secure and overdid certain things, at times lacking insight into the future consequences of my actions. A way this manifested was when I had applied and gained acceptance into a Master's Program for a Counselling Psychology Degree...while I was halfway through my Doctor of Naturopathy Degree program. It was an impulsive decision driven by the fear and anxiety of not trusting in the process of becoming a Naturopathic Doctor (ND). I was so impulsive that I didn't iron out the finances behind this decision. I ended up dropping out in the first semester.

Other ways that I've acted out due my distrust in the process involved being frivolous when it came to investing my attention and time. I prioritized what I enjoyed, going into fitness, teaching, and coaching roles although there were times where it was crucial for me to wholeheartedly attend to what I was studying. Yet, feeling like the unbreakable and undefeatable "Superwoman," I continued on in this manner without fear. To be honest, this was partly due to my underlying intentions of seeing if there were ways to make these interests of mine into bigger careers or side hustles; just in case the ND stuff didn't pan out.

I also suffered from the modern-day disease known as FOMO: fear of missing out. I would try to fit things into my schedule by de-prioritizing things which would've served me better if they were higher on my priority list (had I had a clearer vision). Needless to say, I didn't feel that way then.

For example, I spent considerable pockets of time online dating even though I was meeting people who were not a good fit for me. I lowered my standards to feel like I was having such experiences and not missing out. I was feeling the need to date, and to put in effort and time in increasing the odds of finding a mate during my "good years," which were being gobbled up by my time in school.

Another way I prevented myself from completely immersing myself into the process was when I had thoroughly convinced myself that I wanted to be a financial planner / advisor. I landed a job within a reputable firm, which started immediately after I took my NPLEX II (Naturopathic Physicians Licensing Examinations) licensing exams. I got accepted into a financial firm, and passed all the necessary financial and insurance exams while dealing with lengthy workdays, late nights, and weekends studying. In other words, very little sleep.

Seeking A Savior In Other Humans

Further consequences of my anxiety-fueled decisions that were made seeking refuge from the discomfort of uncertainty involved me looking to be saved. After leaving my role in the financial firm— quite abruptly too—amidst job searching and studying to retake my final licensing exam, I worked a few temporary roles with different employment agencies. One role which seemed to display a bright future filled with potential and excitement involved working as an Administrative Assistant for a business owner. The role promised the possibility of going from part-time to full-time, with possibilities of benefits, perks, and future potential in the industry. However, what I recognize and acknowledge now was my trying to find a way to latch onto the success of the one I was being an Administrative Assistant for, to feel that I could be successful and live my dreams via helping her be successful and achieve her aspirations. I ignored the flashing neon sights standing tall, of underlying agendas unbeknownst to me, which only became clearer as time went on, when actions didn't align with ambitious ideas mentioned prior.

Another example of my seeking a savior would be one regarding my ex: helping him fix, paint, and set up his home, subconsciously thinking that he'd see the investment I was making and would want to naturally extend the efforts to assist me. Proving myself as someone invested in his success, and wanting to be in his life long-term, and holding a significant position amongst his other relationships.

Upon reflection, I can see the ulterior motives that I was bringing into both dynamics. Through being a people-pleaser and aiming to portray my value through how much I could do, I was looking for both of these people to save me. One through elevating my financial status, the other through elevating my self-worth, and both through the expectation of providing me with a sense of security. What a heavy and selfish burden I placed on both of them to bear.

PART 2:

IMPOSTER SYNDROME

Chapter 4

Imposter Syndrome

Harvard review aptly defines imposter syndrome as such: a collection of feelings of inadequacy that persists despite evident success. My personal experience of it surrounds chronic self-doubt and a nuanced sense of intellectual fraudulence—perfectionism's plague, if you will.

I knew I had to eventually resolve the dissonance: to quit battling to show that I am confident versus avoiding attention altogether by not shining as brightly as I could. There were times that I felt intense excitement, and that I have a message worth sharing. During such times, I hold little inhibition and I feel good about my greater purpose. At these times, I'm ready to take on the world. But more often than not, when I'm not in such a state, I succumb to feeling self-conscious about sharing the message rather than being secure in myself; believing that I have what it takes, and I have something to offer; that this world is not limited in its status quo, and that there are people specifically looking for what I have to share and offer.

I buried myself in studying, yet felt as if I haven't worked hard enough. When interacting with others, I couldn't help but feel tested, though many a time they merely seek to provide help in good faith. I was constantly trying to prove myself, and as a result, was oftentimes in situations where competition was self-inflicted, rather than something the situation necessitated. I remember, in during my clinical internship, just wondering if the treatment plans I had created were good enough, and questioning if patients would get positive results (even though it was inevitable if the steps were abided by and executed fairly well).

I was never good enough—not in my eyes, nor my belief.

Why Aren't I Good Enough? And Why Do You Keep Coming Back to ME?

My memory of one of my first patients as an intern remains vivid—from our first appointment onwards, they would constantly ask how they could get connected with the intern they used to see, who had since graduated. Every three weeks, I would provide that doctor's website so that they could see them as requested, but I couldn't help but notice mixed signals. After all, they were still booking appointments and coming to see me, yet repeatedly mentioned their intent to see that practitioner for the same purpose.

So, I really needed to focus on not taking it personally, although each visit meant them stating their preferences for what their previous practitioner would do in comparison to my developing style.

It's important to be understanding of preferences along with industry standards, but it's also a simple matter of being respectful—especially to those now in a position to serve your needs, more so if you're not going to seek help elsewhere. In retrospect, I wish I had been clear in recognizing the purpose I brought and properly separated my values and worthiness which would have enabled to provide even better care. It is only now that I realize that one's role doesn't define them, and that one's value doesn't lie in winning others' approval.

Alas, I didn't know better, and found this critical experience to be challenging. I just felt like I was not measuring up; that I was performing, and not doing very well. I didn't know where I was going, or what I was. I would have loved to have a 24/7 mentor in my back pocket. Someone that I could go to and somehow, help me figure out the apt responses and answers for each and every curveball swung my way.

As you figured, that didn't happen every moment of the day, and I was stuck, knowing that these experiences brought opportunities for learning, but at the same time wondering: why aren't I good enough?

Chapter 5

Busting Out Of The Cocoon But One Wing Gets Stuck

As mentioned, I fear being in the spotlight, and that often came out in spades. When I first started studying Naturopathy back in 2012, I had a colleague that I looked up to who was a few years ahead of me. Every blog post she published, I made sure to read religiously. Her openness and honesty inspired me to share my experience as I felt like there was a lot of information that I would have liked to have heard during the program, and I just wanted to create something that would help others who may have been as lost as I.

I decided to create a YouTube channel, where I shared my journey throughout the Naturopathy program. I figured it'd be useful, seeing that at the time, there wasn't a lot of readily available information online regarding the student experience in this field. I also shared my hair journey in taking care of my natural hair and locs. The problem was that I quit when I didn't have a thick enough skin to deal with non-supportive comments, and that's when my motivation sizzled. It was especially difficult to stomach that some of the most critical and unsupportive discouragements came from people I believed to be rooting for my success. This made me question: am I acting like a clown by being so public? The problem became clear: that I had started these projects to fuel my ego, and to distract myself from what I needed to be focusing on.

Consequences Of Imposter Syndrome

Some ways said consequences ended up manifesting in my life include my failing of courses—not because I didn't know what I was doing, but because I blanked out and would over-study to the point of quadruple-guessing many of my answers. My sleeps were restless, plagued by nightmares, reminding me—in a torturous manner—of how unprepared and incompetent I was.

I overate, I couldn't sleep, I couldn't study, I couldn't think.

Avoid Those Who Aim To Dim Your Shine

I recall speaking to a colleague after I graduated, who, instead of allowing a moment to be congratulatory, instantly said, "I wish I could be where you are." For some that would be a compliment, but I was disappointed. It made me wonder if people can truly be happy for and acknowledge other people overcoming challenges and the hoops they needed to jump through. So, I keep this in mind with anyone I'm talking to who's going through voiced or private challenges. Sometimes one's capacity to genuinely hold space for, to hear and see others, is just not available. I commit myself to remembering that everyone is going through hoops all the time, and to appreciate and acknowledge each individual's conquered plight.

Chapter 6

What's The Point Of Impressing Others?

This was something that I've pondered over from a young age, my curiosity instigated by the adults guiding me through life. Although I know they came from, and continue to come from places of love and concern, I question the intensity of the message I received by some about making sure one looks appropriate wherever one goes, as people are bound to judge one on appearances.

The car you drive needs to look flawless. Your clothes ideally name brand, your shoes always need to be or look new, and you can't wear the same outfits too often (such that others can remember when you last wore them). It was all about appearance, and this idea that you're going to be judged and, in light of that judgement, prohibit yourself from living a good life.

From a young age, that had me feeling vastly insecure about where I stood in this world. I felt like I didn't measure up on my own, and therefore had to put on all these layers and accessories to be noticed and taken seriously. As if being me wasn't enough to stand out.

The Paradox Of Productivity

There's a feeling I feel sometimes—often on Saturday nights—when I'm either feeling overwhelmed by all the projects I've piled on my to-do list, or when there's simply nothing to do. Just this empty, hollow feeling. It's a huge sense of sadness, and I feel all alone in this world. I'd feel this mostly over the weekends, when not having plans for that time of the week. Fridays as well, but mostly Saturday evenings and Sunday afternoons, when I find myself unoccupied. I feel like there are things I should be doing. Like dating, or hanging out with my friends, or at the very least, impose upon myself some form of structure to my day. If I was working on something, I'd feel that I shouldn't be working on it. And if I wasn't working on something, then I'd feel like I should have been. There was this daunting discomfort to just be and just leisure myself in life. I'd feel uncomfortable spending time by myself, as in those moments are where my true insecurities and fears would bubble up—inner demons that I didn't want to acknowledge would then populate. That's when my regrets about certain decisions, and feelings of being trapped and stuck because of said decisions would grab hold of me. I feel this when I'm overwhelmed, and when I'm being "unproductive."

Doing Your Best Doesn't Ensure Security

One of the scariest instances of this feeling occurred when I was laid off during the Covid-19 pandemic. I had just left a job that I had been in for exactly a year, and had left without prospective options lined up after 6 months of job searching. Before the job search, I worked as a temporary part-time hire, to "prove myself" and was then promoted to full-time. Simultaneously, after completing the process required at the time to become licensed and registered in my province as a Naturopathic Doctor (ND), I shifted to working part-time at the other job and started to build my naturopathic practice.

However, I felt extreme financial insecurity based on not having significant funds coming in as an ND, along with my monthly financial obligations for student loans and life expenses. Then, I got hired full-time by another company, in a role that was totally different from anything that I have done. But it was something I really enjoyed—it was based on being detail-oriented and organized, and it was a new challenge that seemed promising. I thought it was exactly what I was looking for at the time.

However, once Covid-19 hit, there were whispers about potential lay-offs coming down the pipeline, and it was noticeably different on the highway with less cars and less congestion. Then, on the last day of my fourth week, I got called in and was told the bad news—I was going to be laid off.

Up to that point, I had never once been laid off, and I really thought that if I had just done my best and brought results and kept learning, kept asking questions, and kept being a great person to be around, that I would not have to worry. It was truly a frightening experience to be told that reality worked otherwise. At this time, I did not have an emergency fund set up and I was not too familiar with the Employment Insurance program, so I didn't know what was going to happen. Luckily, I still lived at home with my family, and feel very blessed and fortunate for that.

It was a very weird time with this feeling of uncertainty the pandemic then entailed. Not knowing how long it's going to play out or how long being unemployed, (and at the crucial beginning phases of being self-employed) would last. And things were still being figured out with regards to any form of government funding. Thus, I was constantly battling between these two thoughts: to start applying for jobs, or to wait it out. Then, the realization that there was no point in applying for jobs at the moment because nobody's hiring due to what's going on hit me. Everything was just going to be delayed anyway.

During that time, uncomfortable thoughts that I would attempt to dismissively push aside made themselves heard with a vengeance. This is where my fears arose, those that questioned me on what I was doing with my life. Maybe if I hadn't gone to school for so long, I would have been at a different job with a higher salary and in a different role where I'm not so disposable. I knew that there was that risk of being hired, yet up to that 3-month mark, being terminated for no reason. So I started to wonder—is there any way to get ahead? It was extremely frustrating.

Just 8 months earlier, I helped my ex set up their new place and thought to myself "I'm going to start taking steps to make this a reality for myself." Yet, there I was. Unemployed, with my insecurities getting too comfortable beside me.

To get laid off after working so hard to learn the role and shifting to adjust, along with not knowing what's going to come next, I was petrified. I felt like I had no control whatsoever despite this life being mine. It then solidified my attitude: I had made a whole lot of wrong decisions with my life.

What this whole experience did solidify was the importance of becoming an entrepreneur, solely so that nobody can ever put me in such a position again—be it intentional or circumstantial. However, one positive thing that came out from it was the steps I then proceeded to take, fueled by a frame of mind that was only possible when pushed to such a corner. If not for this experience, I would not have been able to adopt such a mindset, and would likely have been powerless if I had merely waited up to that point.

Chapter 7

Surrendering To The Unknown

Another period in which I was overcome with emptiness was when I had left the job at the financial firm after all the weeks of finishing my Naturopathic internship, followed by studying for my first attempt of the NPLEX II (Naturopathic Physicians Licensing Examinations) licensing exams, and then a bonus study session for a financial counselling certification I had on the bucket list from a few years prior. The role at the financial firm entailed a daily 62 km one-way commute along one of North America's busiest highways, the 401. At that time, I was also studying for the CSC (Canadian Securities Course), the CPH (Conduct and Practices Handbook), and the LLQP (Life License

Qualification Program). It was such a hectic process, chasing the promise of financial security.

Needless to say, it was a shitty feeling—that which told me this was not the direction I'm meant for, and to throw all of that away. So, there I was, in the middle of applying for other jobs while studying for my second (and what I deemed to be final) attempt of the NPLEX II licensing exams. Not to forget having to put up with waves of flashbacks to the last time I studied so hard, only to await the release of results which was 6 weeks later, which then confirmed my failing of the exams. What if I fail them again?

This was a prime opportunity to express my faith.

During this time, I used the tools I gained when I was completing my certification to become a Certified Life Coach. I also looked over my prayers that have been answered, as I flipped through both my prayer journal, and gratitude journal daily.

You Steer Where You Stare

At the time, I didn't know why I was doing what I was doing. I knew that what I desired was stability and money, and to feel like I was going somewhere and not wandering aimlessly.

I wish I could lay claim to having the much-needed mindset to focus completely, but I honestly had waves of productivity that were constantly interrupted—by nervous breakdowns, and questioning my path in life—feeling like all would be easily conquerable and achievable, especially with God's strength within me. I had tons of questioning moments where I found myself wanting to do something else, and feeling like I was missing out on things.

Where Are The Fruits Of My Labor?

I graduated from a prestigious university in 2012, followed by a super intense post-graduate program...and now it's 2019, the start of a new year. What do I have to show? I studied through the holiday break and that was a reflection of most of my life prior—I had given all these years of studying, for some shape or form of delayed gratification. I wanted a house, I wanted a family of both humans and furry friends. I wanted a stacked savings account and investment portfolio. A trainer and personal chef. I wanted it all. And now, with this exam, there's no guarantee that I'm going to pass. I was at the complete mercy of my plight, and could do nothing but my best and surrender the rest away, to whatever outcome my actions would bring.

PART 3:

DESPERATE FOR VALIDATION

Chapter 8

"Hello, I'm Over Here, Can You See Me?!"

For some reason, I've always felt like I needed to make a unique contribution. I wanted it to be special, and I wanted to garner the attention of others, but at the same time, I wanted to also be seen as providing some sort of help, through being honest and empowering others; providing a voice and solutions, or providing context where there isn't any available.

With the YouTube channel I started in school, I wanted to talk to others about my hair journey of starting locs, and share the story of my naturopathic journey. With regards to the hair journey, it was really meant to encompass a focus on self-love, and acceptance of who we are. My goal was to help others see themselves through my own journey, hopefully depicting—with significant conviction and faith—that it's possible for anyone. To encourage those who reject themselves, to instead, embrace who they are via first embracing their natural hair. The end-goal was simple: to inspire others in the act of embracing the entire journey of nurturing themselves, through both the ups and downs of having their natural hair as-is.

However, the channeling of such content wasn't sustainable. I was too much of an open book. I didn't have a thick enough skin to deal with criticism, and I didn't have enough of the "why" factor, stability, and the perspective of a bigger picture to keep me going. When things became really challenging, this all became crystal clear. I also reached a point of self-realization where it dawned on me that I embarked on this endeavor for wrong reasons—for example, sometimes I would overshare, and in that moment, feel like it is a great thing for me to do so, only to read comments relaying that my intended message was misperceived.

With regards to my venture into fitness, at the time it was focused on bringing attention to physical appearance more than anything else. However, I made sure to also provide an insightful view through the lens of health whenever possible, backed by research, training, and my course of study. I wanted it to be a little like "look at me," but also, "hey, I'm a health expert and you can trust me with what I'm saying." Being a fitness instructor—especially my experience as a Zumba instructor—really increased my love for the human body and movement, along with the building up of endorphins. But what I really loved about Zumba, if I was being painfully honest, was simply being the star.

I loved being at the front of a room. I loved the process of learning the choreography. And I absolutely loved the process of sharing that choreography and excitement with everybody else, and witnessing them picking it up and enjoying the music. I loved being in a place where my body, musicality and creativity were celebrated and encouraged to flourish, all while helping others feel comfortable and—most importantly—entitled to doing the same.

Who—What is God?

There was a time that I was in a rather complex relationship. The longer my relationship with Justin went on, the worse I became. With him, I'd never feel good enough. All too frequently I found I was comparing myself to others and wanting to twist myself into his ideals of what he found attractive. I always felt like I didn't measure up, and I strived to be who and what he desired. I wanted to build myself up to be the representation of what he was seeking.

At the end of the day, I felt wrong to the core. Whenever he would critique me, my focus was on fixing myself. This happened more often than one would think. He would critique my appearance by saying I look tired and withhold compliments. He'd critique my personality by saying that I'm too scared of the world, that I was boring, and over-sensitive. Before plugging the cord, I had morphed into someone else, someone who was very insecure and uncomfortable in her skin. Instead of taking it as a mismatch, I took it as him being immensely strong, and that I needed to strengthen myself in order to get to his level. Instead of striking a balance, where both of us improve and compromise to meet somewhere in the middle, it became more about me needing to find myself, thinking that I was being shaky in the moment, and that I needed to rebuild myself in his image.

I'd be terrified to communicate honestly and to say my truth and to be honest. I'd hide a lot.

I also became very addicted to his attention.

It became a cycle of resentments building up and then wanting to have a conversation about it, but dismissiveness and seduction would temporarily squander the concerns. I wasn't being heard. Then I'd reach a breaking point of threatening to end things and he was fine with it so I would emotionally explode. It would end over and over and over again. Until it was over for good.

It took me turning 31, 8 years of ups and downs, and   therapy   to   leave.

Chapter 9

Bridges and Supports

The very first time that I experienced therapy was when I broke up with my first official boyfriend. At the time, he was the centre of my Universe. I thought we were going to get married after we graduated, and would be happy in our careers and budding family. I was way too ahead of reality. I was devastated because he had broken up with me on Facebook, just before Thanksgiving, no less. My attitude prior to the breakup was one of excitement, that I finally had a boyfriend and people were starting to meet him. The breakup thus came as a huge shock. In fact, he didn't even tell me directly, he just updated his Facebook status. My cousin called me with the news and told me the matter before he did.

I felt like I couldn't deal with life. I couldn't handle it. It was one of the worst feelings ever and I didn't know how to cope. I felt like I was losing my mind and thoughts of an extreme nature would not stop flooding in. What made it worse was his refusal to answer the phone whenever I called. The whole ordeal was torturous.

The great thing about that nightmare is that it led to the first time I sought a therapist. We talked about how the breakup was affecting me emotionally and mentally, and how it was impacting my academics, along with what I really wanted for myself. We also explored my relationships and started the process of drawing parallels between familial relationships, along with expectations of what I consider to be normal within a relationship, and the acceptance of certain behaviors and the rejection of others.

During this time, I was taught the importance of developing self-compassion and how to embrace an acceptance of the situation. This made for a lifelong lesson that I, to this day, continue to learn.

The next time that I went to therapy was when I had been sexually violated by someone. Although I saw the danger, I brushed it off as my mind exaggerating, along with ignoring my desperation to "win" this male over and ended up walking myself into it. Forever grateful that the situation hadn't escalated to a fatal one, this experience brought me back to counselling, and we once again looked at the same relationships. Too often an event with a man, and me not holding my power within his presence, kept landing me in therapy.

And then came the time I was with Justin. At this point, I really started to question myself. Why am I still feeling so devastated over the same patterns that kept happening in my life? Then it really started to click. I need to change certain things in my life as these patterns are repeating, and they're leading me to extreme frustration and unhappiness. I was then—finally—beyond the point of saying "I don't know better" I was ready to take responsibility for my actions.

The beauty of it all was that I got to get connected to different programs, and one of the things I did was self-assertiveness training. It was a group program for 8 weeks with other people who were also dealing with anxiety and depression. We met weekly for group lessons, where we learned about how to be assertive. We discussed people-pleasing, doing things that we didn't really want to do, along with the reasons we felt compelled to and how we felt when we dishonored ourselves.

One of the things I value the most about my undergrad education—aside from it being a time of exploration, extracurricular activities, and structured learning—was the ability to be in an environment where resources were so accessible. Prior to university, in my household, it was not encouraged to seek therapy and to talk about your issues outside of your immediate circle. There was this concern of letting people know your business and of making it look like you don't have it all together, therefore creating cracks in your foundation of living a good life.

In fact, I think this liberating experience really encouraged me to start my YouTube channel because I wanted people to know the importance of accepting yourself and whatever you're going through. Our connecting link is that we're all human. Although we may differ in our beliefs, I believe that—in addition to our physical bodies—we have mental, emotional, and spiritual forces in and around us that transform us from being dead to being alive. As it's important to honor all of these aspects of ourselves, I wanted to use myself as an example to show that: yes, it's terrifying to get out there and be vulnerable. It can also be nerve-wracking to face one's fears and to expand one's self while allowing the world to see. Yet you will see, *you will be okay.*

People are people, and people will continue to be people, regardless of whether it's good or bad, but at the end of the day, you will be okay. I intend to continue to share that underlying message on my current YouTube channel – <u>Eat 'N' Live Free</u>.

Step Out; The Support And Resources You Need Will Appear

For me, one of my biggest pillars of support is God. I was raised in a Seventh-Day Adventist Christian household, where it was encouraged to go to church, and it was one of my favorite things in the world.

I loved going to church with my grandparents, and enjoyed seeing my friends at Sabbath school, while participating in the choir. I loved the community.

Even though I was younger, and didn't know what the pastor was talking about, nor did I have the life experience to relate, I always had this feeling of warmth. Like I was being wrapped in a warm cloud every time I entered the church.

However, once I really got immersed in school, volunteering, and working, church no longer was a big part of my life. Neither was God. I believed in karma, and the idea of doing unto others as you would have one to do to you, and to live and let live—that's how I lived my life. I also became extremely critical, and often wondered how things could happen if there was a just God. For example—how could 9/11 happen? How could slavery happen? How could genocide happen? How can massive power and resource inequalities exist? How does abuse continue to happen? And with university being an intellectually-charged and research-based environment—along with having had the freedom to do what I want and seeing the benefits of working hard, while always feeling like it was all of my dealing—that brought me further away from God.

Fast forward to 2018. I just graduated from the Naturopathic college and I had finished my licensing exams and was door-knocking with a financial firm in the winter. I had encountered several experiences of racism in the low-diversity territory I was in. The most poignant one which occurred was when I heard some people mock Martin Luther King's "I have a dream speech" and made loud comments about their ancestors which made me feel really uncomfortable. I also wondered why the hell I was doing this.

In a tailspin, after spending all this time commuting and studying and door-knocking and not hitting the targets set out by the firm to achieve financial success according to their timeline, I was truly lost. Prior to that, I had started watching Elevation Church; I was searching for a church that felt like home, but I wasn't finding it in my local community, so I proceeded to look online. One day, I was curious, and looked into where the locations were, since they mentioned one in a city near me. I looked it up and found out that it was located at an 8-minute drive from my workplace and from the place I was staying at for my last month of work. So, I decided, on this specific day, that I was going to the church, and go, I did.

That sermon for me was pure magic. It was about "reversing your worry." At that time, I realized that I was just spinning in circles. I didn't know what I was doing with myself. I felt so lost and I didn't know where I was going, why I was doing what I was doing. I was trapped. Trapped by not knowing what decisions to make. Do I redo this licensing exam or do I not? Should I quit this job, or should I keep trying to meet the quotas? What do I do? What do I want to do? And in that moment, I just wanted to believe that there was and is a greater plan for me—one that is uniquely created for me. I don't know what took over me, but in that moment, I said the prayer—I said I'm going to accept Christ, and I'm going to walk with Him.

I felt this amazing feeling of warmth, like I was being hugged, followed by a release of pure emotions while I cried. It was unexplainable, the way that sermon was written. I believe—and will continue to believe—that it was written just for me.

PART 4:

UNCOMFORTABLE IN MY SKIN

Chapter 10

God, Why Did You Make Me This Way?

Sometimes I ask God why He put my spirit in this package. How can He love me with everything that happened to my ancestors? Why couldn't I be born with certain privileges that others are unaware of, and even abuse? Why do I need to be considered inferior? Why are my brothers dying needlessly and brutally, why aren't they given justice? I was— and at times am— pissed that I was born Black, and am floored by the unfair treatment that still exists.

Unattractive, Unworthy

It started when I was younger. I felt unpretty because of my darker skin, and because my guardians constantly fussed over my nappy hair. I was a late bloomer in terms of when I started getting attention from the boys. Needless to say, in my early years I didn't think of myself as pretty, nor did I feel attractive.

I remember wanting to look Caucasian, and straightened my hair in 7th grade after observing the other girls in my class and the actresses in the shows I watched. They would wear their hair by neatly tucking it behind their ears. One Friday evening, after staying up really late, I straightened my hair and attempted to cut the front chunk into bangs. They didn't fall the way I imagined, and they weren't the length they were when I cut them. Wasn't that the purpose of straightening them first? And, as if matters weren't bad enough, my hair smelled burnt even though I had used a protectant and minimal heat.

A middle ground I'd fortunately stumbled across was getting braids, which kept my hair tidy while allowing me to connect with my Afrocentric roots. What's wrong with wanting long hair? I remember feeling the most beautiful in grade 5 when I got braid extensions for the first time. Sitting in the chair for 8 hours in my mom's friend's basement, looking at old braid magazines while she talked on the phone. The moment she dipped the ends in hot water to seal them, was the moment I knew I'd be beautiful. I felt like a bombshell the first 2 weeks of having braids, before they started to look messy. I also remember the excitement when seeing the new growth fray out of the braids, and the act of taking them out to see how much longer my hair had grown in those 8 weeks. Yet, I ended up mortified by all the dead hair which had shed, and was utterly disappointed to see the contrast between the mid back-length extensions I'd wear, and my natural hair, which barely reached my shoulders.

Colorism is something that I noticed from music videos growing up, from the way that Black women were portrayed. There's been, and continues to be these ideas (whether conscious or subliminal) that having fair skin is associated with being more beautiful, and how having certain features (such as a wide nose and nappy hair) make you less attractive. Ergo, the less of that that you have, the more beautiful you are.

During my twenties, while dabbling in online dating, two of my relationships turned into something of some substance, but the other ones felt as though they had this element of exoticism. It was during these days that I learned the pattern and could guess with great accuracy when certain people would make an exit (otherwise known as ghosting). So, being the person that I was, I took this to mean that I'm not worth people staying. That I'm not beautiful enough to keep their attention, along with other messed up ideas.

Hair Journey

From a young age, my hair was constantly fussed over. Before I was able to intervene, it was always ensured that my hair was chemically relaxed so that it would be straight, less kinky, and easier to manage, allowing me to look more "presentable." I remember the hours spent combing it and adopting of a whole plethora of different hairstyles which I didn't feel beautiful in. I usually felt weird about my hair. I would spend hours putting products in my hair to try to make it the same texture as the people surrounding me, and even tried to cut my hair to give myself bangs, which we know turned out to be absolutely disastrous.

Then I met Eva while working for the government. I thought she was absolutely gorgeous with her healthy skin, athleticism, at-the-time short locs, and radiating self-love. I became obsessed with her hair and did some research into the style of locs, and got interested in the whole culture, studying figures like Lauryn Hill. I realized how absolutely beautiful these women were. When I look back, it was clear that seeds were planted by one of my first relationships with a man who saw the inherent natural beauty in Black women. He had suggested I consider loc'ing my hair because I often wore extensions. By then, meeting Eva, and seeing other women and men with locs on YouTube, I saw how beautiful these people were and realized the newfound possibility of having long hair.

So, I did my first big chop during university. At the time, I wasn't planning to loc my hair, but I was sick of how chemically damaged my hair was that I just wanted it gone so that I could start anew. I didn't know what I was going to do about it yet, but I knew that it was severely gross, stringy, and unhealthy, and I just didn't want that on top of my head. So, I went ahead with it and continued to wear extensions.

I did another chop before starting my locs, and that's when I started the YouTube channel. As mentioned before, the goal was to help women to realize that they're beautiful as they are, and that it is possible to have long hair that is natural. I wanted them to see the journey. I became hooked to other people's YouTube channels. It was not just them that I was hooked upon, but their journeys as well, more so, even. I was so inspired that I wanted to start my own adventure and share the experience as well. I bought every book that I could find, and I learned as much as I could. I even considered becoming a loctician! That's how fascinated I had become with locs.

Comparison And Jealousy

This is something that I have strongly struggled with and it is also why I've been trying to carve out my own interest and piece of the world—to nurture and take care of—so that I'm not so overly focused on what other people are doing. In relation to beauty, I've compared myself to all I saw around me. Being jealous was a mere aftermath.

What Are You Hiding Behind That Smile?

There was a time when I considered myself to be a helpless victim to food addiction. When I lived in student housing while completing training in Naturopathy, this was something that I would hide. I would get fast food and hide it in my bag in hopes that nobody could see it, but I'm pretty sure that they could smell it. Also, during my clinic internship, after many of my shifts, I'd get fast food. I felt this helplessness of never being able to stop.

A way I tried to battle this and make it work was through "intermittent fasting." I would cover it up under the idea that intermittent fasting is a good way to give my digestive system a break, but really, it was merely masking itself as an acceptable way to continue my eating disorder since I was doing it for "health reasons." I also had a spending addiction; I was constantly seeking knowledge and just never feeling like I had enough. I thus ended up buying a whole bunch of books and courses with the whole idea that if I gobble up all this knowledge—if I consume all of this—then I can change and I will be

able to have everything that I want and everything
would   be   okay.

Chapter 11

Your Worthiness Does Not Come From What You Do, & For Some, You Will Never Be Enough

There are critical moments in life which tell you who and what you're working with. Where you get a first-class ride into a person's core being, deep beneath the charm and layers of social grooming; when someone is the most honest about who they are, what they believe, and their worldview. And in your soul, on an intuitive level, you know this to be truth, and you can either take it or leave it; your choice.

Although it's vivid in my mind at the time of writing this, I hope that the knife-in-my-heart sensation will fade away with the passing of time; a sensation that overwhelms me whenever I recall

Justin telling me, "*no offense*, but if you don't have $50,000 saved for a down-payment, and you've been living at home even though you graduated two years ago, *you're a waste*."

This was a critical moment for me because I could feel the immense judgment and what seemed to be superiority (or projected inferiority) spewing off of someone I considered to be my partner. I couldn't understand how such a simple sentence, which was said so nonchalantly, was able to have such a strong hold on me to poison my view of myself and make me completely forget about the whole context.

It wasn't until I spoke with my coach about the difficulty in leaving that relationship and the pain I felt from that statement, along with the difficulty to not ruminate on it, that I understood it to be a form of abuse. A violent attack on my worth and usefulness as a human being. And that's where it clicked: I will never measure up to him in his eyes, and I dodged a bullet in that relationship, where it would have been impossible to win.

PART 5:

FROM
OBSTACLES-TO-CURE
TO
BRIDGES-OF-FREEDOM

Superwoman Status Is Overrated

And here we are, coming to an inevitable close. This section will be different in that I'll be sharing 7 lessons which encourage living less like a wannabe superwoman, and in a more "authentic" and self-caring manner. They are inspired by my training, insightful time with clients, and personal life experiences. They also lean heavily upon especially influential paradigms in my life: Naturopathic and Homeopathic Medicine.

When I studied Naturopathic and Homeopathic Medicine, I was drawn to the fundamental principles which shape and inform the treatment philosophy for lifestyle health.

My favorite principle addresses obstacles to cure.

There is a natural direction that things flow when unimpeded. The way a stream flows when a dam isn't blocking the way.

A secure confidence which is developed when one's inner being is nurtured.

A raising of one's vibration when they are surrounding themselves with others who build them up instead of nitpicking at them and tearing them down.

And, of course, the inherent wisdom of our mind, body, and spirit, when supported and not compromised by our environments, thoughts, behaviors, and actions which are misaligned with our values.

Just as addressing the root cause leads us to the necessary treatments (whatever the concern may be), addressing these blockages direct us to what the root cause(s) of any concern may be.

I'm going to suggest alternative attitudes and approaches to life when dealing with not feeling like we measure up. These skillsets are the foundation of my work with my clients, and I remind myself of them on a daily basis.

Note: it takes repeatedly and diligently changing beliefs for people to get to a place where the initial belief no longer rings true.

Through using these principles as tools to build a different reality, I've personally noticed that it's easier to let go of wanting to be a superwoman; easier to let go of having a strong pull that leaves me constantly feeling the need to prove my worth and my value.

I also show myself that I love myself by upholding these boundaries and doing things which align to my values. It can be challenging at times, as my previous nature would have me doing said things, simply because I was trained to believe that that was the right way to do things and to get ahead. Ironically, these principles start with the importance of not striving for perfection. To stray from toxic perfectionism.

Obstacle #1:

Perfectionism

Why is it necessary to be perfect? It's impossible. Also, it's highly stressful.

Striving to be perfect—or as close to it as I could be (not to be confused with my personal best, as opposed to what society deems as unquestionable universal ideals)—fueled my binge eating disorder and spendthrift tendencies. These were my go-tos when it came to coping with the impossibility of achieving such ideals.

There's nothing wrong with wanting to be your personal best; to set your own bars, and to improve in areas that are important to you and will benefit you. But only when it's coming from a place of already being a whole, worthy, and valuable person. Regardless, even then, why try to be perfect? What do you gain from that?

Let me rephrase that, because the external world can be rewarding.

What do you gain internally? And does it come at a loss?

Aside from external validation and rewards, how else does it benefit you to be perfect?

After slowing down and creating space to have this inquiry and reflection within myself, I realized something. Whenever I was striving for perfectionism, it was often for the benefit of other people. Yes, I was trying to be perfect to get to a certain "place," but I was motivated to prove my worth to others so I could get to said place.

Then, I realized: what does it matter anyway? Once I had given all of myself and established super-high and hopeful expectations, I'd end up suffering from being overly invested. It would be even more painful when I was so tied to the outcome, and couldn't get what I wanted from all that effort.

Some things are just not attainable when you are honoring yourself and when being upfront with what your driving desire is. So, are you a failure just because you cannot meet something that's set up to be near impossible?

I think that's really unreasonable. And, at the end of the day, who are you doing it for?

<u>Obstacle #2:</u>

Desiring What Others Have
Instead Of
Focusing On Being Grateful For What You Have

In addition to fundamental health principles, I also draw inspiration from historical and spiritual wisdom. One of my favorite commandments from the Bible is the tenth commandment, which states that we aren't to covet (want to take) others' goods.

This would especially be an issue for me when someone else, who was better than me in a whole range of ways (as we all have our areas of strength, and areas that we can improve), would get what I believed I wanted.

I'd be so consumed by how I imagined how much more complete and happier I'd feel if I could have a certain possession. If I could be with the person I thought I loved, and have him devote his heart instead of his body to me, as have a balance in our dynamic. I'd feel resentful towards the person who had accomplished or attained what I wanted, and viewed the world through the lens of lack instead of abundance. Those feelings weren't fair to them, nor me. We are well suited for our own things, the best of which may differ for us individually.

<u>Obstacle #3:</u>

Stinkin' Thinkin'

I am so grateful to my doctor, who connected me with a therapist when I was on the brink of dropping out of school due to the difficulty I faced in trying to "keep it together," academically and professionally—while dealing with both anxiety and depression, no less. Although we discussed taking a benzodiazepine medication short-term to take the edge off the anxiety to get me through the more stressful academic seasons, what I needed was a different solution.

My therapist and I did cognitive behavioral therapy (CBT) together. CBT is a form of talk therapy which is used to address many mood disorders, eating disorders, and other mental health concerns. The basis of CBT is that our thoughts, feelings, and behaviors are all interconnected, and that by unpacking specific situations which occurred earlier in our lives, we can address maladaptive ways of how we make decisions, thoughts which do not serve us, and sources of feelings which may lead to dishonoring actions and thoughts (and vice versa).

Stinkin' thinkin' is a memorable way to refer to cognitive distortions, which are thought patterns (often automatic), which distort our perception of reality.

Some of the most common types of cognitive distortions are:

- **Should statements** - can contribute to feeling pressure and resentment
- **All-or-none (dichotomous/polarized) thinking** - seeing things as completely one way or another, without an in-between
- **Overgeneralization** - applying one negative experience to all experiences
- **Mislabeling** - extreme overgeneralization when a few traits of someone are generalized to the person as a whole
- **Negative filtering & disqualifying the positive** - focusing on a negative aspect of a situation and disregarding everything else
- **Jumping to conclusions** - arriving at a confirmation without having thorough information. This can be seen as **mind reading** (assuming one knows what another person is thinking) and **fortune telling** (anticipating something is going to turn out negatively)
- **Catastrophizing** - exaggerating insignificant events and assuming the worst is going to happen
- **Minimization** - downplaying significant events
- **Emotional reasoning** - believing that emotions equate to truth, without other evidence
- **Personalization** - assuming things that others say or do are a direct reaction to oneself

This is part of the reason why "should" gives me such a cringey visceral sensation, as mentioned earlier. It brings me back to the deep work I did with my therapist, and I recall how damaging this form of thinking can be.

Stinkin' thinkin' contributes to perfectionism, feelings of worthlessness, anxiety, depression, addictive behaviors, and a whole list of other icky feelings, thereby preventing us from being comfortable and confident with ourselves, and how we relate to others.

If stinkin' thinkin' is something that you notice is disrupting your life, I recommend you check my tools page (www.congratssuperwoman.com), where you can find a therapist who can meet with you virtually. I also encourage you to seek one in your area if it would be of value to you to meet in-person.

To add, for deeper reading on this topic, I encourage you to read my go-tos which have been referenced above: "Feeling Good: The New Mood Therapy" by David Burns, MD, and "Mind Over Mood: Change How You Feel by Changing the Way You Think" by Dennis Greenberger, PhD and Christine A. Padesky, PhD.

<u>Obstacle #4</u>:

Discomfort With Saying "No"
And
Wishy-Washy Boundaries

There is value in saying yes to things that may make you uncomfortable; they encourage you to climb out of your comfort zone and expand your sphere of comfort. However, what I am referring to here is choosing to say "yes" when you know that you want to say "no," but you're saying yes for someone else, rather than for yourself.

There's a difference between being flexible and being an agreeable team player, but when you tune into yourself, it's clear whether the "no" is coming from that place, versus being motivated to people-please, out of a hesitation to rock the boat, or wanting to show that you are capable of handling many things (for the others' benefit more than your own).

This is an obstacle because there's only so much time in a day. There's only so much energy that we have. There's only so many days that we have on this side of life that we're aware of.

So, it's important to think about what you're saying yes and no to, because every time you say yes to one thing, that automatically means you're saying no to something else. Are your decisions serving you? Are they serving your greater vision for yourself? Are they in alignment with your own chartered North Star?

Whenever saying "yes" to something, take a pause to consider the following:

- Do you really want to do this?
- Is this something that's going to benefit you later?
- Is it more for the benefit of somebody else?
- Is it a form of covert manipulation, even though it seems to be coming from a loving place?

Learning to say no has been especially challenging for me. I've been concerned about letting people down, and potentially losing relationships or potential business ventures. My overall fear of losing future opportunities would tie me to a place I would soon realize I didn't want to be in.

However, when I reconnect with and remind myself of what my North star is, the discomfort becomes a transient experience, and I can move forward trusting that I've made the best decision given the info I have at the time. Of course, times may arise where I momentarily doubt a past decision, but then I eventually make peace with the fact that there will always be decisions to be made, or not made, to fill the vacuum of time. I'd rather base my decisions on what my personal values deem being worthy of my time (and accept the consequences), than spend my time doing something I don't really want to.

As previously mentioned, one of the best opportunities my therapist led me to was to participate in an 8-session assertiveness training with other individuals who were also struggling to stand firm in saying "no." There, I learned that, as a result of feeling yanked around by life, and uncertain of ourselves and decision-making capabilities, we were irresolute in our conviction of what to say "yes" versus "no" to. I also learned that inner resentfulness often contributes to depressive moods, while fear of factors and relationships we can't control—despite our best efforts to do so—rev up anxiety levels and disturb our peace.

During the assertive training, I also learned that my relationship to Justin was an obstacle to my mental health and my ability to love myself. A blockage to my peace, a major contributor to insecurities and the constant questioning of my competence of being a human, and worthiness of being connected with him.

We talked about how over-giving I was in the relationship, and my reasons why. And although most of the time it was coming from a place of love, a large intent was to give him reasons to stay and never want to leave. I often did things I didn't want to do. I compromised my values while convincing myself I had a chance with him.

I put his goals above my priorities, so he could see how much I was investing in him. My hope was that he'd naturally desire to reciprocate investing in me. The hardest part was recognizing that, no matter how much I hoped and tried to talk to him about it, his unwillingness to listen nor change meant that I could either continue to expect that, continue to expect different (and torture myself), or say "no" and leave. I'm very proud of him and what he's achieved, but I could no longer exist in a relationship dynamic which came at a health cost to me.

The assertiveness training, alongside learning from my classmates and seeing the patterns through humanity, gave me the strength and knowingness to eventually close that door, and trust that I have the tools to face the difficulty of ending that relationship, yet choose the path of more opportunity for myself with regards to healing. It changed my life.

Basing Your Value And Self-Worth On Your Productivity And Performance

Have you ever felt like if you weren't busy, then you were being unproductive, and, by virtue of being unproductive, you're less valuable as a person?

As mentioned before, I experienced this after graduating from a program I devoted 6 years of my life and the majority of my attention and resources to see through to completion. I felt it after leaving my job at the financial firm, after leaving my role as a dedicated Administrative Assistant, and after resigning my Naturopathic license.

Even though I've had loved ones celebrate all these accomplishments and have gathered these credentials in their eyes, after it was done, and the novelty of completion wore off, I honestly felt kind of useless.

I felt useless because I wasn't seeing things take off as quickly I had expected given the resources I had invested, and effort I had given to generate momentum. I felt useless because so much was up in the air to be decided. It wasn't all in my control. And it didn't bring me the instantaneous and long-lasting happiness I imagined I'd feel when chasing the highs.

Feeling incomplete led me to feel an anxious drive to overproduce. Such as, if I was applying for jobs, I felt I "should" (stinkin' thinkin'!) be applying for everything which was a viable option, all hours of the day, with minimal rest. That if I'm resting, then I'm losing out on potential opportunities. If I didn't pass the licensing exam, then it wouldn't be worth taking over again, and it meant that I wasn't worthy of being in the profession.

As you can see, these catastrophic ways of thinking had a big impact on my value of my sense of self as a person. Yet, what I've learned—and have come to believe—is that my beingness is that of a beautiful creation of God. As a result, I've learned to not base so much of my self-worth and value as a person on what I can produce. This meant, and continues to mean putting boundaries in relationships, what I spend my time on, what I give my attention to, and constantly reminding myself of my bigger picture.

<u>Obstacle #6:</u>

Unclear North Star

What is your North Star? What is important to you? What are your values?

I encourage you to ask yourself these questions when the pressures of the world and the world's timelines are disrupting your sleep, which is supposed to be nourishing and restorative. I often need to remind myself too.

Something else which has helped me in navigating through life is finding my North Star. Some people call it God, or Higher Power, or the Universe.

My North Star is God. And once I found God, it changed my perspective of living on Planet Earth. I started seeing the world as secular versus spiritual. When I accepted myself to be a spiritual being in a physical body, and that there's a spiritual world surrounding me, along with spiritual laws and spiritual principles, I realized I don't have to just take what I'm told from certain sources to be truth. I'm still a seeker, however, shifting my values accordingly helped me in more ways than I can count.

I've become more patient and less frustrated when things don't go the way that I think they "should". It's made me not rush about my life as much, because I believe there is a greater purpose for me, and that it will be achieved.

Obstacle #7:

Thinking You Need To Go It Alone

Another obstacle is the stoic attitude and mindset that you don't need support: whether you think that people can't do things as well as you, and would prefer not to delegate, or, if there's fear in being vulnerable with others who may very well be trustworthy, rooted in previous experiences of trusting those who proved to be otherwise.

As social beings, we're not meant to do everything by ourselves. As much as it is important to have space to tune into ourselves, staying in our heads too long can be counterproductive at times. Also, this especially depends on your default self-talk. So, having a support system—people who are rooting for you, going through similar things as you, have been there/done that and can guide you, people who want to remind you of how truly amazing you are and how you will conquer and succeed and be there for you— is crucial. You are not alone, nor do you need to go it alone.

SUGGESTED RESOURCES

Go to www.congratssuperwoman.com for a list of resources based upon this book's subject matter. You'll also be able to access the reflective worksheet to encourage your inquiry and self-discovery.

Acknowledgements

Thank you to my parents for creating me and bringing me into this world. It takes courage to welcome new life, especially when you're still learning and growing. Thank you for loving me and providing this opportunity!

I'd like to thank my friends and family for all of your support in what I do, and for always rooting for me: Abbah, Aunty Marilyn, Beth, Chante, Chip, Chris, Crystal, Danielle, Donna, Heather, Joanne, JP, Little B (Owen), Melvia, Nadine, Nichele, Robert, Sarah, Yen.

Thank you to my coach, Dr. Andrea Maxim, ND, for showing me the possibility of publishing a book by doing it, and making things happen. I also appreciate you for providing me with the knowledge I needed to build my professional practice when I was feeling stuck and frustrated. You are such an inspiration to me.

I would also like to thank my coach, Goddess Abiola Abrams, for the ability to work with you through your Spiritpreneur Visibility Lab, and to hone in on my book through your Book-Brand-Business course. I am beyond grateful for your guidance with the steps of writing my book, along with coaching me through my fears, and continuing to root for my success. I appreciate you being a source of support for me during one of my most challenging years, and reminding me to journal it out for healing and future inspiration.

Thank you, Bonnie Weiss for the healing and freeing experience of training with you to become a Christian Life Coach. The experience deepened my experience with my Creator and blessed me with tools to support others to do the same. You've also enabled me to connect with such lovely friends whom I am grateful to know.

Thank you, Dr. Shaunna Menard, MD, for helping me to believe that I have something to offer, and that the effectiveness and value of what I have to offer is not dependent upon my title. I appreciate you helping me to package my skills to create my Eat 'N' Live Free - Binge Freedom starter kit, and for bridging me to you through your first book: Free to Heal: 9 Steps to a Successful, Soul-Satisfying Health Coaching Practice. I would like to thank you, as well, for your catch phrase "Be Good For You"... just because you can, doesn't mean you should.

I'd like to also thank my editor Abel Chan for your interest in my project, and for helping me to shape this into something I'm excited to share with others.

I love you all, thank you <3

ABOUT THE AUTHOR

Alisia Young obtained her Honors Bachelor of Science in Health Studies and Psychology from the University of Toronto, and her Doctor of Naturopathy Degree from the Canadian College of Naturopathic Medicine. She also holds certifications as a life coach, eating disorder recovery coach, healthy eating and weight loss coach, fitness instructor, and personal trainer.

As founder of Eat 'N' Live Free, Alisia consolidates her training and experiences to partner with her clients to develop emotional, food, and life freedom, so they can confidently take care of their careers and themselves. Alisia strives to empower high-achieving individuals to recognize the connection between identity, success, and one's health.

In her spare time, Alisia loves learning about other ways to live a life of freedom, and how to build a passive income empire.

Connect with Alisia at:

Instagram: @eatnlivefree
Free Private Facebook Group: Eat 'N' Live Free
Youtube: Eat 'N' Live Free
Email: support@eatnlivefree.com
Website: eatnlivefree.com